How to Start
a
Babies-at-Work
Program

Carla Moquin
Parenting in the Workplace Institute

Additional copies of this book can be purchased at
www.BabiesAtWork.org
or
www.ParentingAtWork.org

If this book has any printing quality problems,
please go to www.Lulu.com for a replacement copy.

ISBN 978-0-6152-4127-2

TEMPLATE POLICY

A full-size customizable template policy and fact sheet (as referenced in this book), including all legal waiver forms for parents and for designated alternate care providers, are available for free download at the site of the **Parenting in the Workplace Institute (www.ParentingAtWork.org/files.html)**.

EBOOK VERSION

This book is also available as an ebook from the **Babies in the Workplace** site (**www.BabiesAtWork.org**) and is free to anyone who has purchased a copy of this book. The ebook contains text links, allows text highlighting and copying, and can be printed. If you wish to obtain your free copy, please contact Carla Moquin at **carla@babiesatwork.org** or (801) 897-8702.

OTHER INFORMATION

Other information relevant to the issues discussed in this book can be found on the **Babies in the Workplace** site (**www.BabiesAtWork.org**).

Table of Contents

How to Propose a Babies-at-Work Program (For Prospective Parents or Others in an Organization)

It is generally most effective to propose a baby program to your organization prior to actually having your baby. The earlier you can start the process of having your company consider the idea, the more likely you are to succeed in your efforts. However, it is possible to start a successful baby program at any point prior to your baby beginning to crawl (most companies with these programs limit them to non-crawling babies up to six to eight months of age).

1. Assess the Feasibility of a Program Where You Work.

Consider your work environment and specific job responsibilities. Your work environment needs to be a safe, stable one in which a sleeping or happily awake baby could comfortably fit. Babies have successfully been brought to work by parents (including a number of fathers) in cubicles, offices, open-plan office spaces, schools, and retail environments including grocery stores, bookstores, and even wineries. The size of your company should not be considered a limitation on the viability of a baby program—baby programs have worked beautifully in companies ranging from three employees to more than 3,000. A listing (sorted by industry as well as alphabetically) of more than 100 organizations that currently allow babies in the workplace can be found in the Baby-Friendly Company List section of the Babies in the Workplace site (www.BabiesAtWork.org).

Babies have been successfully brought to work by people in a wide range of job positions. Babies have been brought by parents who were at desks all day, by parents who were always on the move and in meetings, and by parents who did a lot of both. Babies have also successfully been brought to work by people whose primary job responsibilities involve frequent interactions with customers or clients in person and on the phone (the feasibility of this can depend on how mellow your baby is, though). Positions in which babies have successfully been brought to work include:

- Office and Cubicle Workers
- Credit Union Tellers
- Lawyers and Paralegals
- Secretaries
- Retail Store Employees (including grocery stores)
- Cashiers
- Facilities Managers (who travel between locations)
- Management Consultants
- Logistics Firm Employees
- Call Center Employees
- Chief Operating Officer
- Vice Presidents
- State Employees
- Publishing Company Employees
- Teachers and Administrators in Schools
- Computer Programmers

The primary consideration for whether your position is appropriate for a baby is safety. If you work in an environment in which you are exposed to hazardous chemicals (such as a laboratory) or substances that would present a substantial risk to a baby (hot liquids, etc.), then your position would not be suitable for bringing a baby.

Several manufacturing and distribution companies allow babies in their office areas but not in factory or warehouse environments. If you regularly travel on company business, this may cause liability concerns for your organization if you drive with your baby in the vehicle. However, a number of organizations do allow employees who travel to bring their babies to work; it really comes down to what your organization is comfortable with. If your current position is not suitable for bringing in a baby, consider whether you could temporarily transfer to a different position or location. Several baby-friendly companies temporarily move new parents, when possible, so that they can still bring their babies to work.

If you work in a job in which caring for a baby while working will be too difficult on a daily basis, consider the option of bringing your baby only two or three days a week (or part of each day) and use the other days to get caught up on any work as needed.

2. Informally Survey Support of Other People in the Organization.

Discuss the idea of bringing your baby to work with coworkers or managers who you think would be most receptive to the idea. Having even one additional person on board from the start will greatly increase the likelihood of having a program be implemented (and the more support, the better). By discussing possibilities with your coworkers, you can build a solid base of support to persuade your company to implement the policy. One way to "test the waters" is to mention one of the recent news articles about babies in the workplace programs. There have been dozens of articles, as well as radio and television pieces, in the past six months about the growing numbers of companies adopting baby programs. You can Google pieces (search for "babies at work" by itself or with the name of the publication you're looking for) that were in Time Magazine, People Magazine, USA Today, the Boston Globe, and regional newspapers, as well as pieces on the

Today Show, NBC Nightly News, Fox Business Network, and others. Links to several of the print and television pieces are in the Media section of the Babies in the Workplace site. Print out or offhandedly mention a media piece to a coworker and say that you find the concept interesting, and just see what their response is. Generally speaking, if they say something along the lines of, "Babies don't belong in the workplace," or anything more negative than that, you're probably not going to have much success gaining their support and your best decision would probably be to drop the subject for the moment (to avoid having them develop overt resistance to your plan). However, if their reaction is more along the lines that they don't think it would work for practical reasons (due to concerns such as crying babies or people not getting work done), they may ultimately become a great ally in your efforts. For those people who have practical concerns but are otherwise open-minded about the concept of integrating babies into the workplace, it may be useful to point them to the Parenting in the Workplace Institute's site (www.ParentingAtWork.org) or the Babies in the Workplace site (www.BabiesAtWork.org).

If you have purchased a copy of the book *Babies at Work: Bringing New Life to the Workplace* (which is available on the Babies in the Workplace site), ask if they would be interested in reading it. The book contains extensive quotes, anecdotes, and analysis about how and why structured baby programs work, as well as their many benefits for businesses, families, and society. It is meant to be a persuasive tool for successful proposal and implementation of baby programs. Reading the book yourself before starting the process of proposing a program will give you extensive information with which you can address other people's concerns. The fact sheet and template policy available for free download at the Parenting in the Workplace Institute's site are also useful tools for sharing with coworkers, so as to give them an understanding of the nature of structured baby programs.

4

If other people have questions or concerns that you are not comfortable addressing, feel free to direct them to Carla Moquin of the Parenting in the Workplace Institute (carla@babiesatwork.org or (801) 897-8702). The Institute provides advice on implementation of baby programs.

3.   Suggest a "Pilot" Program as an Alternative.

If your coworker is open to the idea but still hesitant, ask if they would support you in proposing a program on a "pilot" basis. This essentially means setting up a program to test how it works. If it works well, then the company would continue it, but if it doesn't work, then you will either ensure that any problems are quickly resolved or you will support the company in terminating the program. All of the companies that planned in advance and set up formal baby programs (even the ones that considered them "pilot" programs) had success and ended up continuing the program for the long term. However, when you're trying to convince people, they will be more likely to support your efforts if they don't feel "locked in" to the idea if problems were to occur.

4.   Talk First With Immediate Supervisor.

It is generally best to go through channels when you want to actually propose a program. The exception to this would be if you have a close relationship with an executive or top manager whom you have already convinced to support your efforts. In that situation, it is likely to be more effective for the manager or executive to actually propose the program (if they're willing) since they may have more organizational leverage for persuading others.

If you will be the one proposing the program, schedule a time to sit down and talk privately about your proposal. Be prepared to mention other companies similar to yours that have successful programs (using the list of companies on the Babies in the Workplace site). If there are baby-friendly companies on the list in your exact field and you want to talk to people at those companies for their perspective and advice, feel free to contact Carla Moquin of the Parenting in the Workplace Institute for assistance in getting connected to the most appropriate person. Provide your supervisor with a copy of the free fact sheet and customizable template policy available on the Parenting in the Workplace Institute's site. It may be helpful to fill in your organization's name in place of [COMPANY] on the template policy before you do this—it will make it easier for the other person to visualize the policy actually being implemented. Explain the business benefits that come from implementing a baby program (you can find these on the Babies in the Workplace site and the *Babies at Work* book goes into comprehensive detail on them). Direct your supervisor to these resources.

5.   Point Out Benefits For the Company.

Benefits include:

- Parents tend to return to work earlier, which means less downtime and lower costs for covering the parent's workload

- Parents are more focused on their jobs since they are not separated from or worrying about their young babies

- Lower health insurance costs due to easier breastfeeding. Studies have shown that for every 1,000 babies who are not breastfed, there are 2,000 additional doctor visits, 600 more prescriptions, and 200 more hospitalization days. One study found that mothers of formula-fed babies took about twice as many days off work to care for sick children as did mothers of breast-fed babies.

- Improved morale from the presence of happy babies

- Enhanced teamwork and collaboration

- Increased retention and employee recruitment

- Attraction of new customers and increased customer loyalty

Be prepared to answer questions and concerns from your supervisor (they will almost certainly have some). Write down the concerns during the meeting—it shows that you are taking them seriously. If your supervisor is not convinced by the end of the discussion, do not give up. Explain that you need to gather more information and ask if you can have a follow-up discussion. Make sure you have a list of the unresolved concerns. If you cannot find specific answers in the mentioned resources, feel free to directly call or email Carla at the Parenting in the Workplace Institute for assistance or ideas. At each point, try to "keep the door open" for further negotiations—don't insist that a decision be made immediately (when people feel pressured, they are more likely to reject new ideas). The more you show your willingness to effectively address the business concerns that are raised, the more likely your business is to be willing to work with you on the idea. If you wish to do so, you might offer to return to work a few weeks earlier than you had originally planned in exchange for being able to bring your baby with you—this is often very appealing to a company.

6. Parents Proposing a Program Whose Babies Are Already Born.

When discussing a program with personnel at your organization, emphasize the components of your parenting style that correspond to the methods described on the Babies in the Workplace site and in the *Babies at Work* book. If you plan to breastfeed, emphasize that breastfed babies get sick far less often and less severely and are often much more quickly and easily soothed through nursing. If you discuss breastfeeding, emphasize that you will either (depending on your company culture) nurse only in a designated area or be highly discreet when nursing. If you anticipate wearing your baby in a carrier or keeping her on a nursing pillow on your lap much of the time while you're working, emphasize that babies who are kept in physical contact with another person cry far less than the "typical" baby in our culture. If you work in a large organization in which you are around lots of people during the day, point out that babies are very social and can be happy for long periods just watching other people, and emphasize that you will utilize this fact to keep your baby happy and to more easily get work done. If your baby is mellow in general, emphasize this. The key is giving people information to overcome the common belief in our culture that all babies routinely cry for long periods. Point out that babies sleep much of the time in the first six months of life and that you anticipate working very efficiently and productively during your baby's naps to compensate for any down time you might experience when the baby needs a diaper change or a play break. As mentioned above, make sure to illustrate that you have thought through potential problems and have clear plans to prevent any issues, and that you are aware of and sensitive to the needs of the business.

7. Provide Evidence of Success.

When discussing a potential program with coworkers or your supervisor, emphasize that you understand that a program will need to be sustainable for the organization and for your coworkers. Mention that more than 100 organizations in more than 33 states (and some in other countries) already allow babies at work, and that more than 1,300 babies have come to work to date. Explain that evidence from these organizations shows that structured baby programs result in very happy babies, provide extensive benefits for businesses, and are overwhelmingly supported by managers and coworkers after they are implemented. Also emphasize that the baby program would apply *only* to babies up to six to eight months of age (depending on what you're trying to propose) or crawling—basically, focus on the fact that you will be combining baby care and work for a relatively short time. It can also be helpful to mention that most people in current baby-friendly companies were *very* skeptical or resistant to the idea until they saw how well the programs worked in practice, and that now they are enthusiastic supporters.

8. Suggest Discussion With Other Companies.

If, after you have talked at length with your supervisor and tried to address all of their concerns, they are still not persuaded, ask if they would be willing to talk directly with a manager or human resources director in a baby-friendly company to gain their perspective and/or be willing to talk directly to the Parenting in the Workplace Institute to explain their concerns. You can also bring up this option earlier in the discussion if it would be useful. Carla Moquin of the Institute can provide names of men and women, including prior skeptics, at a number of organizations who would be happy to share their knowledge.

If you have gained the support of other employees prior to your discussion(s), it can be better to wait to mention this fact until after you have first discussed the other issues with your supervisor. (Of course, if your supportive coworkers go with you to make the proposal, this doesn't apply.) You don't want to come across as pressuring the supervisor to agree based on other people's support. Coworker support is helpful, but it won't be a critical factor (unless you have a huge number of supporters) until you can first convince the supervisor that the program will be beneficial and successful—and not disruptive—from a business standpoint.

Often, after you have addressed the specifics of how and why baby programs work, as well as their benefits, a supervisor will actually bring up the issue of how other people in the organization might react. At this point, say that you know of several people who have indicated that they are supportive of the idea (you can give their names if they have given you permission to do so), and reinforce the fact that there have been many people in current baby-friendly companies that were very resistant to the idea prior to implementation but became supportive after they saw the program in practice.

If you are unable to convince your supervisor to support your proposal (but assuming that they are not actively hostile toward the idea), a last resort (depending on the nature and size of your organization) may be to consider temporarily moving to a different department. Some larger organizations started a baby program in only one department as a test and then expanded the program to the rest of the company once effective parameters had been established and they knew that the program worked. Depending on your position and job responsibilities, you may be able to temporarily transfer to another section or location of the company during your baby's time at work if you can convince a different supervisor or executive to give the program a chance.

9.   Take the Proposal to Upper Management.

Once you have persuaded your supervisor to support your efforts (or at least to keep an open mind about the idea), get their permission to take the concept to higher levels of the company. If they will join you in that effort or spearhead the proposal themselves, so much the better. Continue persuading people until you have convinced a primary decision-maker to try implementing a program (again, emphasize the "pilot" approach—people will be much more likely to try it as an "experiment" rather than a permanent policy). Another middle-ground approach (if your company is very resistant to the concept) is to propose that the baby initially come only on a part-time basis, perhaps two or three days a week (or even one, to start) instead of on a full-time basis.

Provide the person responsible for implementing the program with the template policy available for download from the Parenting in the Workplace Institute's site and share with them the How to Implement a Babies-at-Work Program (For Management) section of this book. Make it clear that you are available for any questions that may arise during the process of setting up the program.

Bringing Your Baby to Work

1. Figure Out Logistical Issues.

Decide what initial equipment and supplies you will bring to work with your baby. The following is a list of supplies to consider:

- Supply of diapers

- Baby wipes

- Changing pad (depending on availability of diaper changing table)

- Spare change of clothes for the baby

- Spare change of business clothes for you (just in case)

- Extra warm and cool baby clothing (daily workplace temperatures can vary considerably)

- U-shaped nursing pillow (even if you don't plan to breastfeed). Boppy is a high-quality, popular brand— this will keep your baby comfortably nestled and happy against you when you are sitting down.

- Baby carrier for keeping your baby feeling cozy and your hands free, as well as to allow for discreet breastfeeding. A sling or wrap is the healthiest for your baby's physical development, but there are many different types of carriers on the market. Several people who regularly take their babies to work prefer the Moby Wrap; the benefit of wraps in the workplace is that they are highly adjustable, enabling different people to easily hold your baby (at your discretion). Two good online resources for browsing high-quality carriers are (www.WearsTheBaby.com) and (www.TheBabyWearer.com).

- A place for your baby to sleep or play when they are not being held by you or someone else. A number of parents bringing babies to work prefer the Pack 'n Play since it easily fits into cubicles, but there are many options available. However, a large soft blanket (such as fleece) may be all you need to set up a cozy nest for your baby.

- Feeding supplies as appropriate (breast pump, formula, bottles, etc.)

- Several extra pacifiers

- Baby blankets (to give your baby a cozy place to sleep as well as to put on parent and coworker laps while holding the baby)

- Age-appropriate toys

- Diaper pail with a lid and odor-eliminating bags

- Hand sanitizer for parent's desk (if desired)

Optional Items:

Your baby will be happier the more she is held or kept close to another person; however, the following items are additional options for parents to consider. (Note: Never leave your baby unattended in any of these items.)

- Baby swing

- Stroller (assess the width of your workplace hallways before investing in a stroller that may end up being too wide).

- Baby jumper (stationary or one that hangs in a doorway)

- Stationary activity saucer (commonly called an exersaucer)

- Bouncy seat

2. Touch Base With Coworkers.

On your first day bringing your baby to work, email or personally contact coworkers who are in your immediate vicinity or with whom you regularly work. Briefly introduce your baby to them. It can actually be useful to do a semi-formal introduction as you would a colleague—this will subtly encourage your coworkers to think of your baby as someone with whom they can develop an individual connection (just as they would with an adult) and will enhance the "community parenting" effect that develops in baby-friendly companies. Tell your coworkers that you want them to feel comfortable coming to you with any concerns or suggestions for making the babies-at-work experience more effective.

3. Expect a Transition Period.

It will take you a few days to adjust to effectively working while caring for your baby. Don't expect to do everything perfectly the first day, and be patient with yourself and your baby. You will naturally develop efficient routines for getting your work tasks done and keeping your baby happy at the same time, and your coworkers will undoubtedly offer ideas that are likely to make things easier. If possible, establish a relationship with a day care provider before you return to work with your baby. This will enable you to have a backup option in the event that you have to bring the baby part-time or if the baby has an unusually fussy day.

4. Respond Immediately to Your Baby's Requests.

When babies need something, they generally don't scream right away (unless their needs have been repeatedly ignored in the past). They instead first make little whimpering or squeaking sounds. Treat these sounds as being just as important and worthy of attention as full-out crying. Babies always cry for a reason, and the more quickly you meet their needs, the more they will trust you and the more time and energy they will have available for exploring and learning about their world. There is extensive research showing that immediately responding to a baby's cries is ideal for their psychological and physical development and leads to a much stronger attachment (and greater emotional security, confidence, and independence as they get older). Much of this data is described on the Babies in the Workplace site and in the *Babies at Work* book. The more quickly you meet your baby's needs, the more quickly she will be happy and calm again—which translates into more time you will have available for getting your professional work done.

5. General Parenting Tips.

Extensive information about baby development and specific tips and ideas for parents for successfully working with a baby can be found in the *Babies at Work* book, primarily in the "Why It Works" and "Parent Tips" chapters. The more your parenting style overlaps with these methods, the more content your baby is likely to be, enabling you to successfully work while keeping your baby happy and healthy at the same time. The core components of keeping babies happy in the workplace can be summed up as:

- Lots of physical contact and holding of your baby

- Responding immediately to your baby's needs

- Frequent breastfeeding (or enabling sucking—pacifiers are strongly recommended if you're formula-feeding)

- Lots of opportunities for your baby to view and participate in social interactions

6. Relax and Be Open to Other People's Assistance.

In all organizations with structured baby programs, coworkers frequently offer to talk to, help out with, or play with the babies for brief periods. Make the most of these opportunities to let your baby get to know and become comfortable with other people and to learn from the knowledge and experience of your coworkers.

Most importantly, enjoy your time with your baby!

How to Implement a Babies-at-Work Program (For Management)

1. Establish Clear Guidelines and Expectations.

The most critical component of a successful baby program is setting out clear guidelines for parents and coworkers. The better you plan ahead of time, the more smoothly a babies-at-work program will work and the more quickly it will be supported by others in the organization. Informal policies may be sufficient in smaller, close-knit organizations, but it is generally recommended that a written policy be used. A free, customizable template baby policy, including legal waiver forms, can be downloaded at the Parenting in the Workplace Institute's site (www.ParentingAtWork.org/files.html).

Go through the template baby policy and make adjustments as desired to suit your particular structure and organizational layout. The policy itself can be changed or shared as you wish. If you have questions during this process or are uncertain of the rationale for a particular provision, feel free to contact Carla Moquin at the Parenting in the Workplace Institute (carla@babiesatwork.org or (801) 897-8702) for clarification or assistance. There is also a fact sheet about baby programs available for free download from the site.

The most important components for success are:

(1) Parents need to understand that their participation in a baby program is contingent on the baby not being disruptive to the work environment and on parents being able to get their work done.

(2) Coworkers need to understand that they can (although they are *not* expected to or required to) play with the babies for brief periods but need to be conscientious about their work as well.

15

When these parameters are made clear, parents become highly responsive to their babies (resulting in highly content, quiet babies) and coworkers are careful to maintain their own productivity while occasionally playing with or talking with the babies (which also helps to keeps the babies very happy). Extensive information for parents about how to keep babies extremely happy in a work environment is presented in the book *Babies at Work: Bringing New Life to the Workplace*, available at the Babies in the Workplace site at www.BabiesAtWork.org.

2. Designate Where Parents Can Go If a Baby Becomes Fussy or to Breastfeed.

A number of organizations designate a break room or an empty office as a specific location for parents to go for quiet, private breastfeeding or in the event that their baby cries for more than a few seconds. (Although most babies in the workplace are highly content, the *Babies at Work* book contains information and resources for helping unusually fussy babies.) If parents have their own offices, this isn't generally an issue since they can just close their doors, but for open-plan offices and cubicle environments, it can be helpful to designate a location prior to a baby starting to come to work (even if the location changes occasionally).

3. Designate Diaper Changing Logistics.

It is critical to designate in advance where all diapers will be changed (to avoid having parents change their babies in inappropriate locations). Many companies felt that it was worth the small investment to install diaper changing tables in company restrooms. Koala Bear Kare wall-mounted tables are a popular option; most of their styles are less than $200 each.

It is also important to make clear to parents that used diapers need to be kept in a container that completely eliminates odors and that diapers must be taken home or disposed of properly at the end of *every* work day.

4. Present the Program to Personnel.

If you are in a relatively small organization, it can be beneficial to have a company-wide meeting to seek comments and suggestions from all personnel. This will give you an opportunity to explain the company's rationale for starting a baby program and to answer any concerns that people may have about the idea. If you work in a larger organization, send an email or memo announcing the launch of the program.

A sample announcement is below (sections to customize are in all caps and brackets):

[COMPANY] LAUNCHES BABIES-AT-WORK PROGRAM

[COMPANY] announces the launch of a babies-at-work program, effective [DATE]. Under this program, new parents who have been employed in their current position for at least [____ DAYS] and who are in good standing will be eligible to bring their babies to work until the babies are [180 DAYS / 240 DAYS] old or until they begin crawling, whichever comes first. During this time, parents will have the option to have their babies with them (provided the babies are not disruptive to the work environment) while they do their jobs.

In starting this program, we are joining the more than 100 baby-friendly organizations around the country in which more than 1,300 babies have successfully come to work. We believe that this program will provide many benefits to new parents as well as to our organization as a whole. We are basing our program on templates and information provided by the Parenting in the Workplace Institute, a professional organization dedicated to helping organizations to set up sustainable parenting-at-work programs. We request your support (or at least that you keep an open mind) in [COMPANY]'s venture into this next level of supporting families and our community.

There is commonly a brief transition period when these programs are first implemented as new parents adjust to working while caring for their babies. We believe that this will be substantially outweighed by the extensive benefits that will come from integrating happy babies into our work community. We request your patience and welcome your suggestions as we explore how to make this program as effective and rewarding as possible for everyone in the organization.

Parents will be fully responsible for their babies during their time at work and are also responsible for completing their work responsibilities. [COMPANY] understands that other personnel may wish to visit or help out with the babies on an occasional basis. This is permitted as long as work is completed in an effective and efficient manner and that excessive time is not spent playing with the babies instead of working. The parent will have sole discretion as to holding of the baby by other personnel.

A copy of [COMPANY]'s babies-at-work policy is available for your review at [GIVE REFERENCE]. As the program gets underway, we welcome your feedback on ways to improve its effectiveness and benefits.

5.   Pre-Plan With Each Parent.

Prior to a new baby coming to work, set up a meeting with the parent to discuss logistical issues. The following are useful things to address with parents.

- Assess feasibility and safety issues related to the parent's job (if their job is inappropriate for bringing a baby, consider temporarily moving them to a different position so that they can participate in the baby program)

- Determine areas in which the parent believes they might need extra assistance while their baby is at work

- Discuss logistical issues (available quiet room, what furniture the parent wants to bring, what they will do with diapers or other trash, and what they need in terms of a place to nurse or otherwise feed the baby)

- Determine whether the employee plans to return to work full time or part time, and how often the employee plans to have the baby with them at work

- Planned method of feeding the infant (explain benefits of breastfeeding)

- Discuss policy and plans in a meeting with all division employees and the parent—especially including any coworkers that will be in the general vicinity of a baby

- Ensure that backup day care is arranged in the event of an unusually fussy or ill baby

- Assess parent's current workload and any high-stress or intensive projects that may be coming up in the near future that may need more staff allocated to them while the baby is there

- Determine who the parent plans to have as their baby's designated alternate care providers

- Ensure that the parent has read and understands the baby policy and that all legal waiver and agreement forms have been signed by the parent and by all designated alternate care providers

6. Designated Alternate Care Providers.

It is strongly recommended that Designated Alternate Care Providers be established prior to each baby starting to come to work (forms for these designated providers to sign are in the downloadable template policy at the Parenting in the Workplace Institute's site). These alternate providers are chosen by parents in advance; they are coworkers who *offer* to be available to care for a baby in the event that a parent is unable to stay with the baby for a brief period of time (such as visiting the restroom) or if the parent needs to attend a client meeting or other event at which the baby might not be appropriate. (However, parents should *never* leave the company premises without taking their baby with them.) Companies generally set a limit on the total amount of time a designated care provider can spend watching a baby in the course of a given day.

Companies sometimes have concerns that, if specific alternate providers are designated, those people will be unduly burdened with baby care. The companies that use a designated care system, however, have not had any problems with parents or alternate providers exploiting the system. Designating specific people in advance who voluntarily agree to help with the babies has a number of benefits:

- Enables parents to feel secure that, if they have an urgent meeting or situation, they have a plan in place for what to do with their baby

- Prevents situations in which parents panic if faced with an urgent situation and beg their nearest coworker to hold the baby, who is likely to feel compelled to agree even if they are not comfortable doing so (which could then result in resentment or tension)

- Prevents situations in which parents in management inappropriately ask a subordinate to take care of the baby, which again could lead to the other person agreeing out of fear of job consequences if they refuse

Even though other coworkers are likely to ask to hold the babies, make it clear that parents have sole discretion in this regard. Also, parents should never ask anyone to help with or hold the baby who is not a designated alternate care provider. This will prevent situations in which people feel pressured to help but don't really want to do so. It is helpful to give parents the option to designate additional care providers if they wish (again, this must be a purely voluntary role on the part of the coworker) during the baby's tenure at work.

7. Baby-Free Zones and Complaint Procedure.

A number of organizations have a provision for a "baby-free zone" if a coworker is distracted by a baby's presence or simply uncomfortable being around babies (this can occur, for example, if an employee is trying to have children but has so far been unsuccessful). If a request is made under this provision, either the parent's or the coworker's work area is temporarily moved for the duration of the baby's time in the workplace (this should be discussed privately with all affected parties to find a solution that is amenable to everyone). This provision is likely to be rarely—if ever—used, but it increases initial acceptance among employees to have the option be available.

A complaint procedure (consistent with other company policies related to grievances) should also be put into place so that employees feel they have options in the event that a particular baby is too distracting, a parent behaves inappropriately, or the parent is not effectively performing work duties. Again, once the program is established and people get to know the babies and see how well these programs work in practice, complaints are likely to be rare or nonexistent, but it is beneficial to provide this option so that people know that they do have recourse if a problem occurs.

8. Publicizing the Program.

Companies that allow babies in the workplace have found that their customers and clients overwhelmingly love the program and love seeing the babies (in those organizations in which the babies are in public view). The media also tends to be fascinated with these programs. If you hope to get positive publicity for your baby program, wait to send out a press release until the program has been in place for several weeks (to work out any last-minute specifics). Most of the media pieces about these programs involve pictures or video of babies at work, so it's best to have your program running as smoothly as possible before inviting the cameras in.

If you have customers or clients coming on-site, it can be useful to create a notice or sign to inform them about your babies-at-work program. For example, one credit union has a sign that is placed at the parent-teller's station while their baby is coming to work. A sample notice (sections to customize are in all caps and brackets) could say:

BABIES-AT-WORK PROGRAM PARTICIPANT

This [EMPLOYEE / PERSON] is a participant in [COMPANY'S] babies-at-work program. [COMPANY] allows personnel to bring their babies to work until they [ARE SIX MONTHS OLD / ARE EIGHT MONTHS OLD / BEGIN TO CRAWL]. [COMPANY] implemented this program in [YEAR] as part of our continuing efforts to support our employees and to ensure that they are at their best for providing the best possible customer service. We have had [TOTAL NUMBER] babies join us to date. We welcome your thoughts on this program.

---

9.   Be Flexible.

Just as in any situation involving people, situations will occasionally arise that have not been explicitly addressed in advance. Be willing to address and resolve those situations on a case-by-case basis, and don't hesitate to tweak the official baby policy provisions over time.

10. Enjoy the Benefits.

In structured programs, babies are overwhelmingly content and the programs are overwhelmingly supported by parents, coworkers, and management. Once you have your program in place, sit back and enjoy watching the positive transformation that occurs in your organization when happy babies enter the picture.

MOVING FORWARD

This book was designed to be used in conjunction with the book *Babies at Work: Bringing New Life to the Workplace* (available through either of the websites listed below). *Babies at Work* provides extensive information about successful baby programs and detailed advice on making them work.

Please note that the forms described in this book (and included in reduced size on the following pages) are available for free download from the Parenting in the Workplace Institute's site (www.ParentingAtWork.org).

If you have questions or require further assistance, please contact:

> Carla Moquin
> Parenting in the Workplace Institute
> 39 Edwards Street
> Framingham, MA 01701
>
> (801) 897-8702
> carla@babiesatwork.org
>
> www.BabiesAtWork.org
> www.ParentingAtWork.org

I hope that this book has been useful in your efforts to implement a baby program in your organization. I welcome suggestions for additions to this book or ideas for furthering our work. Thank you for your efforts to help the workplace become more baby-friendly.

> Carla Moquin, President
> Parenting in the Workplace Institute
> August 1, 2008

A reduced-size template babies-at-work policy and a fact sheet about baby programs are on the following pages.

A full-size policy (designed to be printed on 8.5" x 11" paper) can be downloaded from the website of the **Parenting in the Workplace Institute (www.ParentingAtWork.org/files.html).**

[COMPANY]
INFANT-AT-WORK PROGRAM

[SAMPLE POLICY TEMPLATE]

NOTE: These documents are not meant to substitute for legal advice. If you have any concerns about legal issues, please directly consult an attorney.

[COMPANY]
INFANT-AT-WORK
PROGRAM GUIDELINES

Policy

It is the policy of [COMPANY] to provide a positive work environment that recognizes parents' responsibilities to their jobs and to their infants by acknowledging that, when an infant is able to stay with a parent, this benefits the family, the employer, and society. The [COMPANY] Infant-at-Work Program encourages new mothers or fathers to return to work sooner by allowing the new parents to bring their infant to work with them until the child [is 180 days old / 240 days old] or begins to crawl, whichever comes first.

Eligibility

Parents – Full-time and part-time [COMPANY] employees are eligible to participate in the program, subject to the specific job responsibilities of the parent and subject to ensuring the physical safety of the infant. Employees currently involved in disciplinary action and employees who have not completed their ___-day orientation/probation period are not eligible to participate. Employees may request a temporary, alternative work assignment if their current assignment is not suitable for participation in the program. [COMPANY] will attempt to accommodate such requests based on business and staffing situations at the time of the request but is not required to meet said requests.

Infants – Infants of part-time and full-time employees [up to the age of 180 days old / 240 days old / until the infant begins to crawl] are eligible for the program, subject to the provisions of these Guidelines.

Alternate Care Providers – Parent must select two other [COMPANY] employees to provide back-up care for the infant. An alternate care provider may not simultaneously participate in the program as a parent bringing his or her baby to work and as an alternate care provider for another parent's child.

Forms to Complete

The following forms are required for participation in the program:

- Individual Plan, which outlines the specifics of the infant's care plan (Attachment 1)
- Parent Agreement, Consent & Waiver forms (Attachment 2)
- Alternate Care Provider Agreement (Attachment 3)

The parent will submit all completed and signed forms to the human resources manager, who will then schedule the Pre-Program Meeting.

Pre-Program Meeting

Before any infant is brought into the workplace, a meeting must take place between the parent and the human resources manager. Both parties must review, discuss, and approve the proposed Individual Plan.

Requirements for Care Providers

A parent participating in this program may not leave the building (not even for a short time) without taking the infant with them.

The parent will accept complete responsibility for the safety of the infant. If the parent's duties require that they leave their primary work site, the parent will take the infant with them. An employee may not take the infant anywhere in a [COMPANY] vehicle.

The parent must provide all supplies and equipment needed to care for the infant at the work site and ensure that the area is kept in a clean and sanitary condition. Diapers must be changed only in a designated restroom or in quiet room locations and not in work areas. When an infant accompanies a parent to work, used cloth diapers must be stored in a closed container and taken home daily. Used disposable diapers must be wrapped appropriately and discarded in an appropriate container provided by the parent and placed in an area not used by staff for office or meeting space. All other supplies utilized by the parent must be maintained in a manner that is not disruptive to the work of other employees.

Parents must have day care or other arrangements in place by the time their baby [is 180 days old / 240 days old / begins to crawl].

There may be work circumstances that require a parent's full attention such that it may be necessary for parents to make other arrangements for child care during these periods. Parents are expected to work closely with their supervisor and coworkers to ensure that all parties involved are aware of what duties can and cannot be reassigned and parents are expected to make alternate child care arrangements when required to do so.

In order for an infant-at-work program to be most effective, all parties need to be sensitive to the needs of others. The employee must maintain acceptable work performance and ensure that the presence of the infant does not create any office disturbances. If problems arise that cannot be resolved, the employee understands that the program may be terminated for that employee.

If a baby is fussy for a prolonged period of time, causing a distraction in the workplace or preventing the parent from accomplishing required work, the parent shall remove the infant from the workplace. The parent will be charged for time away from work according to leave time provisions of [COMPANY] or may be subject to pay deductions for missed work.

[COMPANY] will identify one or more locations on the premises that employees may use, if they so choose, while breastfeeding or otherwise feeding their infants.

Infant's Location During the Program

Work Station – Each parent shall make her/his workstation suitable for the new baby and the baby shall be located primarily at that workstation during the work day. [COMPANY] will make every effort to offer a privacy office, if needed, but can not guarantee it if space constraints make this infeasible.

Quiet Room – In the event that an infant becomes noticeably fussy, loud, or uncontrollable, or exhibits any behavior that causes a distraction in the workplace or prevents the parent from accomplishing work, the parent must immediately take the infant to a sitting room until the infant calms down and is quieter. If the infant does not calm down within 30 minutes while in the sitting room, the parent must remove the infant from [COMPANY] premises.

Other Employees – The infant may be in another employee's workspace for brief intervals if the arrangement is agreed upon between the parent and the other employee. Consideration must be taken to ensure that the environment is safe for the infant at all times and that other employees are not disturbed.

Illness

A sick infant should not be brought to work. If the infant becomes sick during the day, the infant must be taken home by the parent. The Center for Disease Control ("CDC") "Recommendations for Inclusion or Exclusion" of children from out-of-home child care settings are attached hereto as Attachment 4, and are hereby adopted by [COMPANY] as a means for determining whether a baby is sick.

Alternate Care Providers

The parent shall choose two alternate care providers who will care for the infant if the parent needs to attend a meeting, work with a customer, go to the restroom, etc. Each care provider will have previously signed an Alternate Care Provider Agreement form (Attachment 3).

If a parent is going to be unable to care for their child at work for a period of less than 1.5 hours within a 4-hour period, the parent shall notify a care provider and place the infant in the provider's care.

If the parent is going to be unable to care for their child at work for a period exceeding 1.5 hours within a 4-hour period, the parent shall make arrangements for the infant's care outside the [COMPANY] premises. A care provider in the workplace shall not be permitted to care for an infant for a period exceeding 1.5 hours within any 4-hour period.

Other Personnel Caring for Infant

[COMPANY] understands that other personnel may ask the parent for permission to care for the infant for brief periods of time. This is acceptable at the discretion of the parent as long as the productivity of other personnel is not substantially reduced. Only the designated care providers should be asked to watch the infant if the parent is unable to care for the infant for a prolonged period of time (not to exceed 1.5 hours within any 4-hour period).

Complaints

All complaints must be made directly to the parent's immediate supervisor, department manager, or the human resources manager, by such means as may be provided. All complaints will be kept anonymous to the extent that is possible. The employee, the immediate supervisor, the department manager, and the human resources manager shall have final discretion to decide what should be done to resolve the complaint. (See Termination of Eligibility below.)

Termination of Eligibility

Parents have the right to terminate their individual agreement at any time. [COMPANY] has the right to terminate an individual agreement at any time if parent's performance declines or if organizational needs are not being met (i.e., complaints and/or disruptions to coworkers cannot be resolved). The employee must maintain acceptable work performance and ensure that the presence of the infant does not create any office disturbances.

This agreement may also be terminated if the parent becomes involved in disciplinary action, if the parent does not comply with the terms and conditions of their Individual Plan, or when complaints have been made that cannot be resolved. Eligibility may also be terminated at the sole discretion of [COMPANY] for reasons not yet known at this time. When eligibility is terminated, the infant must be removed from the workplace. Depending on the circumstances, [COMPANY] may require immediate removal or notice may be given.

Other

The [COMPANY] Infant-at-Work Program is a voluntary option for employees, subject to approval as outlined in these Guidelines, where it is compatible with job requirements.

Other affected employees may request a "baby-free" work environment. Such requests should be made through the employee's immediate supervisor and the human resources department. [COMPANY] will attempt to accommodate such requests based on business and staffing situations at the time of the request.

Participation in the [COMPANY] Infant-at-Work Program is a privilege and not a right.

[COMPANY] expressly reserves the right to refuse participation in the Program for any reason or no reason at all or to terminate participation in the program due to business conditions or for no reason at all.

[COMPANY] expressly reserves the right to change or revise this policy with or without notice.

ATTACHMENT 1
[COMPANY]
INFANT-AT-WORK PROGRAM
INDIVIDUAL PLAN

GENERAL INFORMATION

Name of Parent/Employee_____ Home Phone_____
Name of Infant_____ Infant's Date of Birth_____
Date Infant Enters Program_____
Estimated Date Infant Will Leave Program_____
Days and Times Infant Will be Present in the Workplace

ALTERNATE CARE PROVIDERS

The following employees have agreed to be alternate care providers, who will provide care for my infant when I am unavailable (not to exceed 1.5 hours within a 4-hour period).

#1_____ (Name)
#2_____ (Name)

Note: If you are on flexible hours, your care providers must work the same schedule that you do.

SPECIFIC INFORMATION

Include any other specific plan information or requirements in the space below (optional):

_____
_____
_____
_____

IN CASE OF EMERGENCY, PLEASE CONTACT:

Name_____
Relationship_____
Home Phone_____
Work Phone_____
Cell Phone_____

Name_____
Relationship_____
Home Phone_____
Work Phone_____
Cell Phone_____

I UNDERSTAND THAT THIS PLAN HAS NOT BEEN APPROVED UNTIL I HAVE MET WITH THE HUMAN RESOURCES MANAGER. I UNDERSTAND THAT, IF ANYTHING ABOUT MY PLAN CHANGES, I WILL NEED TO MEET ONCE AGAIN WITH THE HUMAN RESOURCES MANAGER TO DISCUSS THE CHANGES AND TO GET MY NEW PLAN APPROVED.

Submitted by:

_____   _____
Signature of Parent/Employee   Date

Approved by:

_____   _____
Immediate Supervisor   Date

_____   _____
Department Manager   Date

_____   _____
Human Resources Manager   Date

PLEASE ATTACH YOUR SIGNED ALTERNATE CARE PROVIDER AGREEMENTS TO THIS INDIVIDUAL PLAN.

ATTACHMENT 2
[COMPANY]
INFANT-AT-WORK PROGRAM
PARENT AGREEMENT, CONSENT & WAIVER

AGREEMENT

By signing this Agreement, I certify that I have read the Infant-at-Work Program Guidelines. I understand and agree to comply with the terms and conditions set forth in the Program Guidelines. I further understand and agree that, in the event I fail to comply with such terms and conditions or otherwise fail to meet any Program criteria (whether or not such criteria are set forth in these guidelines), my Program eligibility may be terminated, requiring me to remove my baby from the workplace with or without notice.

I acknowledge that [COMPANY] is offering participation in the Infant-at-Work Program as a courtesy to part-time and full-time employees who are new mothers and fathers, and that it is not an employee benefit. Accordingly, I further acknowledge that [COMPANY] reserves the right to terminate a participant's eligibility, with or without cause, or to cancel or retire the Program in part or in its entirety, with or without cause, at any time, thus requiring me to remove my baby from the workplace, with or without notice.

_____   _____
Signature of Parent   Date

CONSENT AND WAIVER

In consideration of [COMPANY]'s permitting me to bring my child to work with me in compliance with the infant-at-work policy, I hereby release, on my own behalf and on behalf of my child, _____: (i) [COMPANY]; (ii) any entity affiliated with [COMPANY]; and (iii) any of the current or former owners, officers, directors, agents, employees, representatives, insurers, attorneys, successors, and assigns of [COMPANY] and the foregoing entities from any and all claims, liabilities, causes of action and demands of any kind or character, including negligence, whether vicarious, derivative or direct, that I, _____, or any of my child's family members, heirs, or assigns now have or may hereafter have or assert against [COMPANY] growing out of, resulting from, or connected with this policy and/or with me bringing my child to work or his/her presence at work with me.

_____   _____
Signature of Parent   Date

33

ATTACHMENT 3
[COMPANY] INFANT-AT-WORK PROGRAM
ALTERNATE CARE PROVIDER AGREEMENT

As a care provider, I understand and agree to the following:

I understand that being a care provider does not relieve me of my responsibilities as an employee of [COMPANY]. By signing this Agreement, I certify that I have read the Infant-at-Work Policy Guidelines. I understand and agree to comply with the terms and conditions set forth in the Policy Guidelines.

When necessary, I will provide care for _____ (infant's name) when _____ (parent) is unavailable. My care will not exceed 1.5 hours within any 4-hour period.

As a care provider, I know I must work the same hours as the infant's mother or father, so I must have the same work schedule that they have.

I understand that I must obtain my immediate supervisor's, as well as my department manager's, approval to participate in this program.

If the infant becomes disruptive to other employees, I will take the infant to a designated quiet room area.

I understand that the parent may not leave the infant in my care if he/she is going to leave the building.

I understand that there is another designated care provider, _____ (name), whom I may contact for assistance.

I understand that no other persons besides the parent, myself, and the other designated provider are responsible for the baby once the baby has been placed in my care. If another employee asks to take the baby, I will first get the parent's approval.

If I should decide that I no longer wish to be a care provider, I will give the parent at least two weeks notice.

I ACKNOWLEDGE THAT I HAVE READ, UNDERSTAND, AND AGREE TO THE TERMS OF THIS ALTERNATE CARE PROVIDER AGREEMENT.

_____   _____
Signature of Alternate Care Provider   Date

_____   _____
Signature of Supervisor   Date

_____   _____
Signature of Department Manager   Date

ATTACHMENT 4

Recommendations for Inclusion or Exclusion
[From the Center for Disease Control (CDC)]

Mild illness is very common among children, and most children should not be excluded from their usual source of care for common respiratory and gastrointestinal illness of mild severity. Infectious disease prevention and control strategies are often influenced by the fact that asymptomatically infected persons can transmit certain infectious microorganisms to others. Parents of children in childcare and adult child caregivers should be educated as to the infectious disease risks of childcare. Following common sense hygienic practices can reduce much illness risk.

Exclusion of children from out-of-home childcare settings has been recommended for illnesses known to be transmitted among, by, and to children when exclusion of the child or adult has a potential for reducing the likelihood of secondary cases. Exclusion has also been recommended in cases of serious illness for which a hypothetical risk of transmission exists, but for which data at present is insufficient to quantify the risk. In many situations, the expertise of the program's medical consultant and the responsible local and state public health authorities are helpful in determining the benefits and risks of excluding children from their usual care program.

Child and caregiver-specific exclusion policies reflect the present state of knowledge. Children need not be excluded for a minor illness unless any of the following exists:

- The illness prevents the child from participating comfortably in program activities.
- The illness results in a greater care need than the childcare staff can provide without compromising the health and safety of the other children.
- The child has any of the following conditions: fever, unusual lethargy, irritability, persistent crying, difficult breathing, or other signs of possible severe illness.
- Diarrhea (defined as an increased number of stools compared with the child's normal pattern, with increased stool water and/or decreased form) that is not contained by diapers or toilet use.
- Vomiting two or more times in the previous 24 hours, unless the vomiting is determined to be due to a non-communicable condition and the child is not in danger of dehydration.
- Mouth sores associated with an inability of the child to control his/her saliva, unless the child's physician or local health department authority states that the child is noninfectious.
- Rash with fever or behavior change, until a physician has determined the illness not to be a communicable disease.
- Purulent conjunctivitis (defined as pink or red conjunctiva with white or yellow eye discharge, often with matted eyelids after sleep and eye pain or redness of the eyelids or skin surrounding the eye), until examined by a physician and approved for readmission, with or without treatment.
- Tuberculosis, until the child's physician or local health department authority states that the child is noninfectious.
- Impetigo, until 24 hours after treatment has been initiated.
- Streptococcal pharyngitis, until 24 hours after treatment has been initiated and until the child has been afebrile for 24 hours.
- Head lice (pediculosis), until the morning after the first treatment.
- Scabies, until after treatment has been completed.
- Varicella, until the sixth day after the onset of rash or sooner if all lesions have dried and crusted.
- Pertussis (which is confirmed by laboratory or suspected based on symptoms of the illness or because of cough onset within 14 days of having face-to-face contact with a person in a household or classroom who has a laboratory-confirmed case of pertussis), until 5 days of appropriate antibiotic therapy (currently: erythromycin) has been completed (total course of treatment is 14 days).
- Mumps, until 9 days after onset of parotid gland swelling.
- Hepatitis A virus infection, until one week after onset of illness and jaundice, if present, has disappeared or until passive immunoprophylaxis (immune serum globulin) has been administered to appropriate children and staff in the program, as directed by the responsible health department.

Certain conditions do not constitute a prior reason for excluding a child from childcare unless the child would be excluded by the above criteria or the disease is determined by a health authority to contribute to transmission of the illness at the program. These conditions include the following: a symptomatic excretion of an enteropathogen; nonpurulent conjunctivitis (defined as pink conjunctiva with a clear, watery eye discharge and without fever, eye pain, or eyelid redness); rash without fever and without behavior change; cytomegalovirus infection; hepatitis B virus carrier state; and HIV infection.

[P][I][WI] Parenting in the Workplace Institute

39 Edwards Street, Framingham, MA 01701
(801) 897-8702
www.babiesatwork.org   www.parentingatwork.org

BABIES AT WORK FACT SHEET

MORE THAN 1,300 BABIES IN
MORE THAN 100 ORGANIZATIONS
HAVE BEEN SUCCESSFULLY BROUGHT TO WORK.

Baby programs have been successful in office-based,
cubicle-based, open-plan, and retail environments.

Baby programs have been successful in companies
ranging from 3 employees to 3,000 employees.

Baby programs require minimal investment and provide extensive benefits.

BENEFITS FOR BUSINESSES

Employees Return to Work Sooner	Increased Employee Recruitment
Increased Retention / Lower Turnover Costs	Increased Loyalty from Existing Customers
Higher Morale and Productivity	Babies Attract New Customers
Increased Teamwork and Collaboration	Low Startup and Implementation Costs
Lower Health Costs From Increased Breastfeeding Rates	Low Liability Risks

BENEFITS FOR FAMILIES

Increased Bonding	Easier Breastfeeding
Financial Stability	Lower Day Care Costs
Socialized Babies	Lower Stress for Parents
Social Network / Support for Parents	Responsive Care Means Happier Babies and Parents
Enables Working Fathers to be More Involved With Their Babies	More Options for Women

ORGANIZATIONS WITH SUCCESSFUL BABY PROGRAMS

Consulting Firms	Credit Unions	Design Firms
Government Agencies	Law Firms	Retail Stores
Manufacturing Companies	Non-Profits	Publishing Companies
Public Relations Firms	Schools	Software Companies

REQUIREMENTS FOR SUCCESS

(1) Clear policy guidelines for parents and coworkers.
(2) Limiting the program to babies who are not yet mobile.
(3) Limiting the program to babies who are content in the work environment and to parents who are able to simultaneously complete job tasks while caring for their babies. It is rare that a situation occurs in which management needs to intervene, but it is critical to long-term success that the company be willing to do so as appropriate.

BABY PROGRAM DETAILS

Babies in structured programs tend to be overwhelmingly content. This is due to four major factors:

(1) High levels of social interaction for babies due to occasional visits by coworkers.
(2) High levels of physical contact for the babies from parents and coworkers.
(3) High rates of breastfeeding, which results in healthier babies who are easier to soothe.
(4) Highly responsive care of babies by parents to avoid disturbing coworkers, resulting in psychologically healthy and highly content babies.

Parents are very motivated to make these programs work.

When there are clear guidelines that babies cannot disrupt the work environment, parents tend to meet their babies' needs at the first whimper, which results in happy babies that cry very little. Parents also tend to work very hard to get work tasks done to ensure that they will be permitted to continue bringing their babies to work.

Babies are highly social and seek interaction with other people in order to learn.

Babies crave information and interaction with other people. In many workplaces, babies have a variety of people to observe and interact with throughout the day, which satisfies their need for social stimulation and helps to keeps them content.

Many people were highly resistant to baby programs prior to implementation.

People in structured programs invariably become supporters after implementation. People (including many prior skeptics) frequently comment on how being around happy babies lowers their stress levels and how much it helps to get a "baby fix" when they are having a bad day.

QUOTES FROM BABY-FRIENDLY COMPANIES

"When they first announced it—when it went live—I was thinking, 'That's ridiculous. How do they expect me to run a branch with babies?' I just couldn't see it working. But they sold me on the program, and I've been really happy with it."

Fran Oswald, Branch Manager
Schools Financial Credit Union (39 babies so far)

"The first time the baby program was proposed at UNCLE Credit Union at the executive level, I said no. I didn't want babies on the teller line because of the coins and other issues. But, the second time the topic came up, proponents of the idea convinced me, and now I am one of the biggest supporters of it. Other companies have had hesitation in deciding to start a program. I'm the best one to talk to; my advice is to try it out. If it doesn't work, you can always take it away. But the benefits of the program far outweigh the negatives."

Wendy Zanotelli, COO
UNCLE Credit Union (19 babies so far)

Parenting in the Workplace Institute

The largest obstacles to widespread implementation of parenting-at-work programs are (1) lack of awareness of their viability and benefits and (2) lack of knowledge about how to set up an effective program and address potential problems. The Parenting in the Workplace Institute is devoted to overcoming those obstacles through extensive grassroots outreach and media coverage about the viability of babies-at-work programs and programs involving older children, as well as by creating and disseminating "best practices" documentation to enable organizations to easily and inexpensively implement sustainable programs.

The Institute's website currently offers a downloadable fact sheet about babies-at-work programs and a template policy that combines the most effective provisions from organizations with successful programs. We are working on other materials, such as a guide for parents on working with a baby and a summary sheet of the benefits for businesses. The Institute provides direct assistance— including email and telephone support—to organizations and individuals wishing to set up new baby programs as well as to organizations with existing programs that wish to increase the sustainability or effectiveness of their policies. As we grow, we anticipate providing on-site support to organizations as applicable. We welcome your ideas for furthering our work, would love to hear your stories about parenting in the workplace, and would love to know about any organizations (worldwide) that currently allow parenting in the workplace. Our ever-growing database of companies with active programs can be found on our Baby-Friendly Company List on the Babies in the Workplace site (www.BabiesAtWork.org).

Institute Contact Information:

Parenting in the Workplace Institute
39 Edwards Street
Framingham, MA 01701
(801) 897-8702
carla@babiesatwork.org
www.BabiesAtWork.org
www.ParentingAtWork.org

About the Author

Carla Moquin lives in Massachusetts, is 31 years old, and is raising two wonderful daughters who are 3 and nearly 7 years of age, respectively. She has a bachelor's degree in psychology from the Pennsylvania State University, a master's-level certification in mediation and facilitation skills from the University of Utah, and was on the Dean's List during her three years of attendance at Concord University School of Law. Ms. Moquin has been researching babies-at-work programs since 2005. She is the founder and president of the Parenting in the Workplace Institute (www.ParentingAtWork.org), based in Framingham, Massachusetts. She maintains the blog Working With Kids (www.WorkingWithKids.org) about integrating children into society. Ms. Moquin has been the spokesperson for the Institute in more than a dozen live and recorded radio and television interviews, as well as for several print articles about babies-at-work programs.

Ms. Moquin conducts ongoing research on baby development and methods for raising babies and children to enable them to be healthy, happy, and to successfully integrate into society. She hopes to spend the rest of her professional life educating and providing resources for sustainable parenting-at-work programs around the world.